Welcome

Hey there, ninjas. I'm Anxious Ninja and this is my activity book. It's packed with everything from fill-in fun to coloring, puzzles, and games.

This book belongs to

....

....

If you get anxious like I do, this is the book for you!

DO YOU GET ANXIOUS FEELINGS?

Many people feel anxious sometimes—and there are lots of things you can do to help manage your worries! Inside this book, you'll discover new ways to deal with your emotions, so you can face the world with confidence. As well as awesome activities, you'll find mindful techniques and breathing exercises to try out, too. They can be your secret weapons to manage your emotions!

Contents

HELLO WORLD!

Grab your pens and pencils to fill in these pages with everything about YOU!

?

My name is ....

My birthday in on ....

I am .... years old

I live in ....

I live with ....

....

....

3 words that describe me:

I would like to be:
(circle your choices)

louder / quieter

funnier / more serious

more athletic /
more creative

stronger / kinder

neater / messier

a better listener /
more chatty

Color them in!

My favorite colors are . . .

This is what
I look like.

DRAW YOURSELF IN
THE FRAME, THEN
COLOR IT IN.

Ninja Life Hacks®

All about me!

My dream job:

- ☐ Astronaut
- ☐ Doctor
- ☐ Writer
- ☐ Teacher
- ☐ Musician
- ☐ Engineer
- ☐ Farmer
- ☐ Firefighter
- ☐ Artist
- ☐ Other . . . .

My best friends are . . .

....
....
....
....

3 unexpected facts about me:

My favorite snack is . . .

DRAW HERE

~~~~~~

My favorite animal is . . .

DRAW HERE

BE POSITIVE! THINKING ABOUT THE THINGS THAT MAKE YOU SPECIAL IS GOOD FOR YOU!

All about me!

Check the things you like to do in your spare time!

- ☐ Reading
- ☐ Crafting
- ☐ Playing sports
- ☐ Swimming
- ☐ Watching TV
- ☐ Hanging out with friends

My favorite things:

Animal: ....

Subject: ....

Sport: ....

Song: ....

Flower: ....

Person: ....

Movie: ....

5 THINGS THAT MAKE ME ANXIOUS:

1 ....

2 ....

3 ....

4 ....

5 ....

5 THINGS THAT MAKE ME LAUGH:

1 ....

2 ....

3 ....

4 ....

5 ....

5 THINGS THAT BUG ME:

1 ....

2 ....

3 ....

4 ....

5 ....

RECOGNIZE THE SIGNS

It's normal to feel anxious sometimes, but the earlier you can spot the signs, the sooner you can look for ways to take care of yourself before anxiety grows bigger.

IT'S A GOOD IDEA TO ACKNOWLEDGE AND ACCEPT ANXIOUS FEELINGS. PRETENDING THEY'RE NOT HAPPENING WON'T MAKE THEM GO AWAY!

How do you feel when you're anxious? Check the options below or write your own in the spaces.

☐ I struggle to concentrate

☐ I feel overwhelmed by small tasks

☐ I don't want to talk to anybody

....

....

....

How is your sleep?

☐ I wake up more in the night

☐ Restless

☐ I struggle to fall to sleep

....

....

....

What happens to your body when you're anxious?

☐ I start to ache

☐ I feel tense

☐ I struggle to relax or sleep

....
....
....

Take a look at what you've filled in and pick one or two to focus on. Think about what you can do about them! Perhaps if you're struggling to sleep you could have a relaxing bath before bedtime, or if you're feeling tense you could do some stretches.

Things to try:

Things to try:

Things to try:

WORRY TREE

Color in this tree in your brightest colors, then follow the steps to work through your worries or anxious feelings!

Put the worry away

Decide what to do and do it

Decide what to do about it and schedule it

Put the worry away for now

Now

Later

No

Yes

Can I do something about it?

IMAGINE PUTTING THE WORRY INSIDE A BOX AND STORING IT AWAY FOR ANOTHER TIME!

What is the worry about?

How did this activity make YOU feel?

Add a thumbs up or a thumbs down sticker here.

START HERE

I am worried

MAKE A WORRY JAR

Write down your worries on pieces of paper, fold them up, put them in a jar, and close the lid. Choose ten minutes each day to open the jar, pick a piece of paper, and talk about your worry with someone you trust.

YOU WILL NEED:

- [ ] A grown-up helper
- [ ] A jar with a lid
- [ ] Small pieces of paper
- [ ] A pen

DECORATE THE JAR ANY WAY YOU LIKE TO MAKE IT LOOK AWESOME! YOU CAN EVEN USE YOUR STICKERS!

I'm Worry Ninja and I like putting my worries in a Worry Jar!

THE 3 Rs

Gritty Ninja is teaching Anxious Ninja a special hack to use when anxious feelings threaten to take over. It's called the 3 Rs: Recognize, Relax, Refocus. Color in each ninja, then try out the 3 Rs exercise next time you start to feel anxious.

You don't have to be controlled by anxious feelings. YOU hold the power to manage your anxiety!

THE 3 Rs CAN BE YOUR SECRET WEAPON AGAINST ANXIETY!

WORD SEARCH

How many anxious words can you spot in this grid? Check off each word as you spot it, then draw a line though it to make it disappear. You've got this!

```
Y U N E A S Y J I K O L X W T
U S B N J U D S A R S U I O L
M B T C F R T H J U C L G R E
Q E T R O P L U H G A C X R W
F R Y J E M U O P G R Y U I X
A W E T U S N V C F E K G E S
E G J K L A S D F E D U J D Z
A W Q T G H U E J A B G D S A
Q V B N Z F R S D R O N V F T
Y R E S T L E S S F D S A X N
J K F H F Y R E S U Z H I N M
K O I U T R O U B L E D O V F
E N E R V O U S G N M H T Y J
P K N I H V T F C Z A S F T U
A N X I O U S V W H K I Q J K
```

- ☐ ANXIOUS
- ☐ WORRIED
- ☐ STRESSED
- ☐ TROUBLED
- ☐ SCARED
- ☐ UNSURE
- ☐ FEARFUL
- ☐ NERVOUS
- ☐ UNEASY
- ☐ RESTLESS

How did this activity make YOU feel?

Add a thumbs up or a thumbs down sticker here.

MY SAFE PLACE

Imagine a very special place where you feel safe and happy. Draw a picture of it here, then color it in using happy, bright colors.

WHEN YOU START TO GET ANXIOUS, PICTURE YOUR SAFE PLACE IN YOUR MIND. IT CAN HELP YOU TO FEEL CALM!

Color in the words that describe the way your safe place makes you feel. Can you think of any other words? Write them in the space at the bottom of the page.

CALM

RELAXED   HAPPY

EMPOWERED

AWESOME   CHEERY

POSITIVE

SAFE   ENERGETIC

SUPER SENSES

When anxious feelings start to take control of your body, focus on your five senses, one by one, to help you stay in the moment and stop your emotions from taking over.

WHEN YOU FEEL ANXIOUS, TAKE A MOMENT TO THINK, THEN FILL IN THE LISTS ON THE OPPOSITE PAGE.

What can you see?

· ·

· ·

· ·

· ·

· ·

What can you hear?

· ·

· ·

· ·

· ·

· ·

What can you feel?

· ·

· ·

· ·

· ·

· ·

YOU DON'T NEED PAPER AND A PEN TO DO THIS ACTIVITY. YOU CAN DO IT ANYWHERE, ANYTIME. JUST MAKE LISTS IN YOUR HEAD!

How did this activity make YOU feel?

Add a thumbs up or a thumbs down sticker here.

What can you smell?

· ·

· ·

· ·

· ·

· ·

What can you taste?

· ·

· ·

· ·

· ·

· ·

LET'S DANCE

Dancing is a great way to chase your worries away! Practice these cool ninja moves, then put them in any order to create your very own dance routines.

Here's a routine to get you started:
1 2 3 4 1 2 3 4 11

1 Jumping jack

2 Point to the right

3 Point to the left

4 Make a heart shape

5 Skip on the spot

6 March to the left

7 March to the right

8 Drop to the floor

9 Reach down low to the left

10 Reach down low to the right

11 Make a wave

12 Tiptoe along

DON'T FORGET! DANCING IS EVEN MORE FUN WITH FRIENDS!

COLOR AND STICK

Match the letters in the color key to the pictures and color them in, then add the correct emblem sticker to each ninja.

Anxious Ninja

Gritty Ninja

Positive Ninja

COLOR KEY

A   B   C

D   E   F

SILLY FACES

Draw a picture of your worried face, looking in the mirror to help you. Now cheer yourself up by adding funny accessories, such as a silly hat, sunglasses, or a moustache.

Draw your picture here.

SPOT THE DIFFERENCE

Learning to keep anxiety under control helped Anxious Ninja to win a race!

Can you spot eight differences between these two pictures of the race?

Add a trophy sticker for every difference that you spot.

LET'S TALK!

Draw pictures of two people you trust, then fill in worries you could talk to each of them about. For example, who would you talk to about homework or friendship troubles?

I'm Communication Ninja! Talking about problems will help you to feel better!

Name: . . . .

We can talk about: . . . .
. . . .
. . . .

Name: . . . .

We can talk about: . . . .
. . . .
. . . .

BLOWN AWAY

Write down things that make you feel nervous in the falling leaves, then close your eyes and imagine the wind blowing them away.

Meeting new people

How did this activity make YOU feel?

Add a thumbs up or a thumbs down sticker here.

Anxious Ninja has done one for you!

DOT-TO-DOT

Connect the dots to finish this picture of Anxious Ninja, then add the worried face emblem sticker and color in your creation.

DRAW IT!

If your worries were an object or a creature, what would it look like? Draw a picture of it here.

MAYBE YOUR WORRIES LOOK LIKE A HUGE RAIN CLOUD, AN ANGRY BEAR, OR A BIG, HEAVY ROCK?

My worries don't look as scary when I draw them!

TAKE A DEEP BREATH

Doing breathing exercises is a great way to calm your body and your mind. Why not try out some of them next time you feel worried or anxious?

Stressed Ninja

1 Lie flat on your back and put a soft toy on your belly. Breathe in slowly and deeply, watching the toy rise. Then breathe out slowly and watch it sink back down. Repeat as many times as you like.

2 Pretend to smell a flower and breathe in deeply, taking lots of air into your lungs. Hold for one second, then breathe out slowly through your nose. Repeat.

Healthy Ninja

3 Use a bubble blowing kit to practice blowing big bubbles. When you focus your mind on what you are doing, you are focusing on the present moment! It's a great way to release built-up anxiety or anger.

Angry Ninja

4 Breathe in through your nose for three seconds, hold for one second, then breathe out through your mouth while making a hissing noise, like a snake.

HISSSSSSSSSS!

Feelings Ninja

ADD A THUMBS UP STICKER NEXT TO THE EXERCISE YOU LIKE THE MOST AND A THUMBS DOWN STICKER NEXT TO THE ONE YOU LIKE THE LEAST.

WORRY JOURNAL

Writing down worries can help to clear your head and make you feel less stressed. Keep a worry journal for a week, noting down all the things that are bothering you.

MONDAY

TUESDAY

WEDNESDAY

SOMETIMES, WHEN YOU SEE YOUR WORRIES WRITTEN DOWN, THEY DON'T SEEM SO BAD!

THURSDAY

FRIDAY

SATURDAY

SUNDAY

How did this activity make YOU feel?

Add a thumbs up or a thumbs down sticker here.

LET IT GO

Positive Ninja knows that there are two kinds of worries—ones that we can do something about (like being late) and ones that we can't (like rain on a day out). Write down any worries you can think of that you CAN'T do anything about.

I always try to let go of worries I can't do anything about!

NOW CROSS OUT YOUR WORRIES WITH A PEN OR PENCIL TO MAKE THEM FLOAT AWAY!

MAKE A STRESS BALL

Make a stress ball to use when you feel anxious, following these simple steps. Just give it a squeeze to help your body relax and release tension.

YOU WILL NEED:

- [ ] A grown-up helper
- [ ] An empty plastic bottle
- [ ] A small balloon
- [ ] A bag of flour
- [ ] A funnel
- [ ] A marker (to draw on balloon)

HOW TO MAKE IT:

1. Put the funnel in the top of the empty bottle and carefully pour in the flour.

2. Blow up the balloon about halfway.

3. Carefully stretch the end of the balloon over the top of the bottle to seal it.

4. Shake the bottle to pour in the flour.

5. Pinch the end of the balloon, remove it from the bottle, then slowly let out the air.

6. When the balloon has deflated, tie a knot at the end to hold in the flour.

7. Draw a face on your stress ball!

How did this activity make YOU feel?

Add a thumbs up or a thumbs down sticker here. →

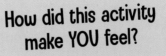

SEARCH AND FIND

Being active always helps Anxious Ninja to feel better. How many of each item in the panel can you spot in the big picture? Fill in the answers in the circles above the little pictures.

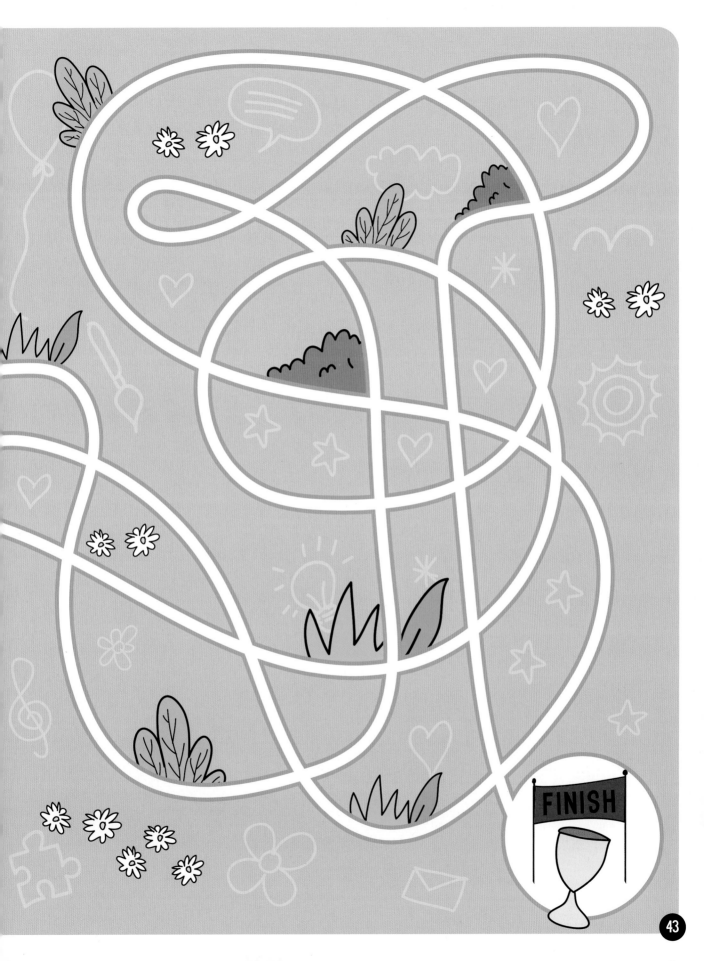

FINISH

WORD SEARCH

When you feel anxious, does your heart beat faster? Do your hands and knees shake? Anxious feelings can affect different parts of your body. Can you find these 12 parts of the body hidden in the grid?

```
Q R Y I P L H F S A E X C V B
N M J Y L U N G S C V A Y U R
E I O L N B C D E R T G R B A
C X A Q W D F H H Q R U P S I
K A X V N M K G W E C B F R N
J M L O L T F C A Q A T Y L H
F V B F E E T N F D E R H J K
Z A W G G P L M F T E S T H Y
U A Z X S V E Y E S B E S X V
N J I F H Y E Q A F H L M H X
F T H I J N K L H S C B H A U
O B E L L Y D E E H N M A N G
Y I A G D S Q F A K O P T D V
X S D T H J U T D X A R M S L
P T E D V M J T F A Z E T U O
```

- LUNGS
- LEGS
- HANDS
- ARMS
- FEET
- HEART
- BELLY
- BRAIN
- HEAD
- EYES
- NECK
- EARS

Check off the words as you find them in the grid!

MAKE A MANTRA TELLER

Anxious Ninja uses positive self-talk, or mantras, to help build up confidence. Follow these simple steps to make your own mantra teller and find your happy place!

How to make it:
1. Carefully cut along the dashed lines.
2. Turn it over to color in the pattern.
3. Fold along the solid lines, as shown in the instructions on the next page.

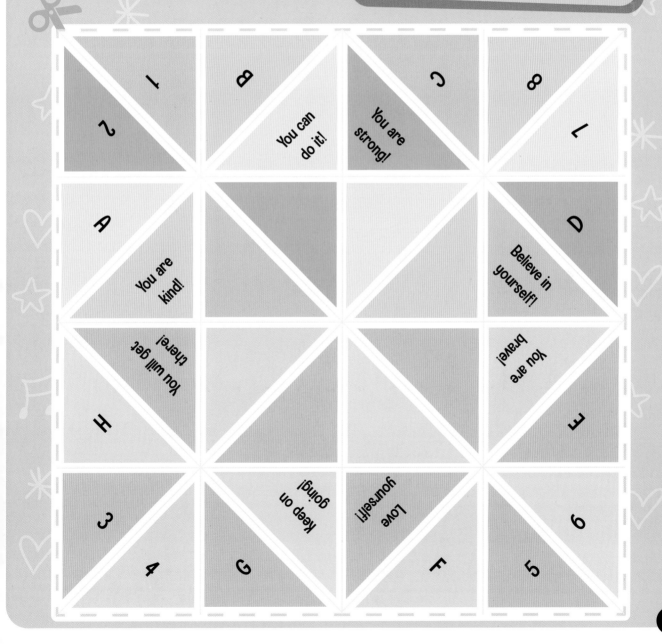

1. Start with the printed side, facedown. Fold the square in half. Then fold it into a smaller triangle.

2. Unfold it so it looks like this.

3. Fold the corners into the center.

4. Flip the paper over.

5. Fold the corners into the center again.

6. Your paper should look like this.

7. Put your thumbs and pointer fingers under the 4 corners to open and close it. Your teller is now ready to use.

8. Ask a friend to choose a number, then open and close the teller that same number of times. Ask them to pick a letter, then lift the flap to reveal their mantra.

SPOT THE DIFFERENCE

Anxious Ninja is going for a walk in the park to relax. There are eight differences between these two pictures. Circle the differences as you spot them.

WONDERFUL NATURE

Anxious Ninja loves interacting with nature. It's a great way to chill if you are feeling uptight. Fill this page with beautiful things found in nature. They can be things you've seen in real life or things you'd like to see.

You could draw leaves, stones, feathers, birds, or bugs.

If you don't want to draw, try to describe things found in nature with words!

Perhaps you've always wanted to see an animal from a different country. Draw it or write about it here.

What's your favorite flower, plant, or tree? Draw it or write about it here.

How did this activity make YOU feel?

Add a thumbs up or a thumbs down sticker here.

CLOUD CREATIONS

Just looking up at the sky can help you connect with nature and de-stress. Doodle to turn each cloud into a different animal or object. Then color in your creations using your favorite colors.

How about turning one into a sheep or a fluffy cat?

ME TIME!

It's important to show yourself some love! Anxious Ninja has lots of ideas for finding a little "me time." Check each suggestion when you try it.

☐ SIT SOMEWHERE QUIET	☐ GO FOR A WALK	☐ CLEAN YOUR ROOM
☐ PRACTICE A HOBBY YOU LOVE	☐ Write a list of all the things that went well this week	☐ WATCH YOUR FAVORITE MOVIE
☐ PLANT A FLOWER	☐ DRAW, COLOR, OR PAINT	☐ Write a gratitude list—what are you grateful for?

SPEAK TO
A FRIEND

DO SOMETHING
CRAFTY

LOOK
THROUGH OLD
PHOTOS

LISTEN
TO MUSIC

Read a book
you've never
read before

WRITE IN
YOUR
JOURNAL

BAKE
SOMETHING
DELICIOUS

DO YOU HAVE ANY
SPECIAL REWARDS YOU
LOVE TO GIVE YOURSELF?
WRITE THEM IN THE
BLANK SPACES.

ANXIOUS VERSUS CALM

Your mind and body can feel totally different when you are anxious compared to when you are calm. Color in the raindrops with the things you experience when you're anxious. Color in the sunbursts with experiences you have when you're calm. There's an empty spot on each page to write other feelings you have, too.

It's hard to sleep at night

My hands shake

I can't stop thinking about the thing that is worrying me

I find it hard to focus on tasks

My heart beats very fast

Color the raindrops with your anxious feelings!

I breathe too fast

I feel like I am not in control

Can you decode this secret message to help fight anxious feelings? Each colored number represents a different letter. Use the key to help you break the code.

9	8	7	6
A	B	C	D
5	4	3	2
E	F	G	H
1	9	8	7
I	J	K	L
6	5	4	3
M	N	O	P
2	1	9	8
Q	R	S	T
7	6	5	4
U	V	W	X
3	2		
Y	Z		

8 9 8 5
_ _ _ _

9
_

6 5 5 3
_ _ _ _

8 1 5 9 8 2
_ _ _ _ _ _

8 4
_ _

1 5 7 9 4
_ _ _ _ _

YOU CAN USE THE CODE TO WRITE YOUR OWN SECRET MESSAGES, TOO!

FAVORITE THINGS

Surrounding yourself with all of your favorite things can help to make you feel safe, secure, and less anxious. Create a colorful poster on the opposite page filled with the things you love. You can use some of the ideas below as inspiration or come up with your own!

Food

Movie

Weather

Flower

People

Animal

Place

Season

Book

Toy

Color

Why don't you pick three things to inspire you?

DON'T FEEL LIKE DRAWING? WRITE ABOUT YOUR FAVES INSTEAD!

Ninja Life Hacks®

How did this activity make YOU feel?

Add a thumbs up or a thumbs down sticker here.

ODD ONE OUT

Puzzles are an awesome mindfulness activity. They can be a fun way to focus your mind and you'll feel a great sense of achievement when you complete them.

CIRCLE THE ODD ONE OUT IN EACH ROW. GOOD LUCK!

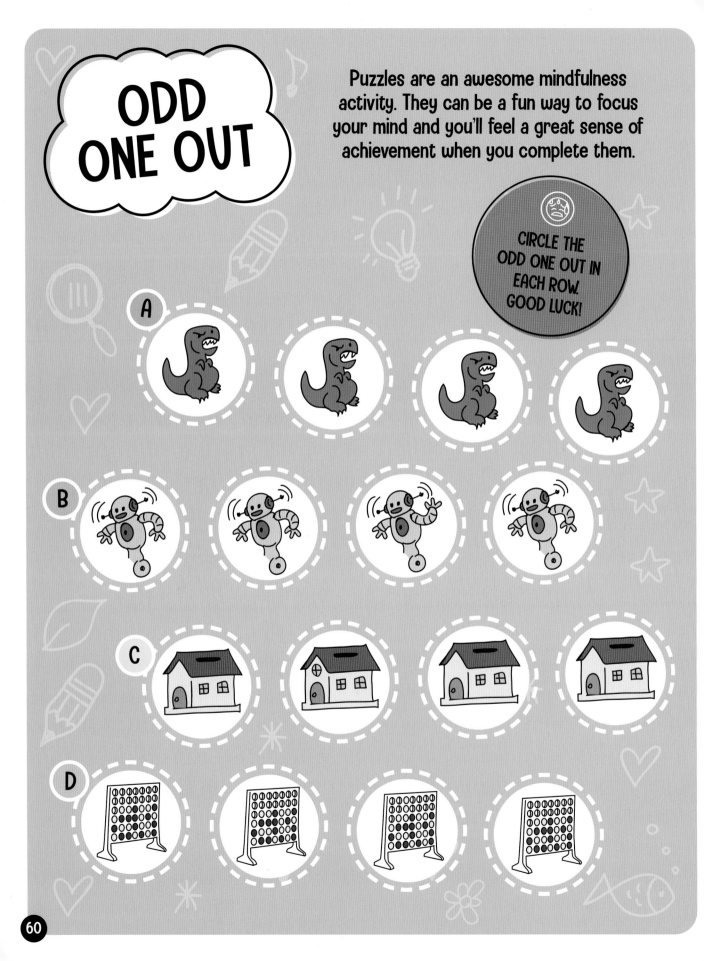

SHADOW MATCHING

Practicing your favorite hobby can help to eliminate anxiety and leave you feeling great! These noisy ninjas are playing their musical instruments. Can you match each one up to their shadow?

DRAW LINES TO MATCH UP EACH NINJA TO THE CORRECT SHADOW.

How did this activity make YOU feel?

Add a thumbs up or a thumbs down sticker here.

DAYDREAMING

Color in this dreamy scene with colored pencils, crayons, or markers. As you color, imagine yourself floating on these fluffy clouds and feeling super calm!

MANTRA-MAKER

Making up your own mantra and repeating it back to yourself every day can be very empowering. Try writing your own mantras on this page, using the hints to help you.

MY MANTRAS

....

....

....

....

....

....

....

....

....

....

YOU COULD USE SOME OF THE SUGGESTIONS BELOW, OR MAKE UP YOUR OWN!

HANDY HINTS

I AM . . . (kind / smart / funny)

I CAN . . . (do this / handle it)

I WILL . . . (do my best / get through this)

WRITE SOME OF YOUR FAVORITE MANTRAS ON A PIECE OF PAPER AND KEEP THEM NEXT TO YOUR BED OR IN YOUR BACKPACK. THEY CAN BE YOUR SECRET WEAPONS WHEN YOU FEEL DISCOURAGED.

COLOR BY NUMBERS

Spending time outdoors is a good way to relieve anxiety and stress. Use the key to help you color in this picture of Grateful Ninja enjoying some fresh air.

COLOR KEY

A   B   C   D

E   F   G   H

LAUGHTER IS KEY

They say laughter is the best medicine! Have fun writing down all the things that make you giggle. Then whenever you're feeling anxious or down, just turn to these pages to cheer you up!

My favorite funny animals are:

. . . .

. . . .

. . . .

. . . .

The funniest TV shows
I've ever seen are:

. . . .

. . . .

. . . .

. . . .

Books that make me laugh are:

. . . .

. . . .

. . . .

. . . .

The funniest movies I've ever
seen are: . . . .

. . . .

. . . .

. . . .

I'm Funny Ninja.
I love to make people laugh!
It makes everyone feel
good, including me!

The funniest person in my family is:

. . . .

Why? . . . .

. . . .

. . . .

. . . .

My most hilarious friend is:

. . . .

Why? . . . .

. . . .

. . . .

. . . .

This is my favorite joke:

. . . .

. . . .

. . . .

. . . .

. . . .

LOL!

CHILL OUT

Anxious Ninja relaxes by listening to music, reading, and playing with building blocks. Color the last item in each row in the correct colors to complete the sequence.

A

B

C

DOT-TO-DOT

Going on a bike ride is the perfect way to get rid of negative energy. Connect the dots to see Gritty Ninja zooming around.

START HERE!

COLOR IN THE PICTURE USING THIS GUIDE TO HELP YOU.

MINDFULNESS MESSAGE

Design your own mindfulness message to go on a tote bag! Use lots of colors to make it stand out.

YOU WANT YOUR DESIGN TO BE EYE-CATCHING AND BOLD SO THAT PEOPLE CAN READ IT AS YOU WALK BY.

Ninja Life Hacks

CALM AND COLLECTED!

Organized Ninja feels most calm when collecting interesting things. Color in the picture of this proud ninja's cool collections.

MINDFUL COLORING

Grab your colored pencils, crayons, or markers and do some mindful coloring! Use as many colors as you like to complete these repeated patterns.

TAKING TIME OUT TO COLOUR IS A GREAT WAY TO REFOCUS YOUR MIND. IT GIVES YOUR BRAIN A CHANCE TO REST, WHICH IS A LOT LIKE MEDITATING!

Calm activities like this one helped me earn my name—Calm Ninja!

SILLY DRESS UP

Sometimes a little silliness can be the best way to relieve anxiety! Draw and add stickers to dress up the ninjas in funny outfits and accessories.

Anxious Ninja

RANK THEM FROM 1 TO 5 IN ORDER OF YOUR FAVORITE OUTFIT.

Pefect Ninja

Organized Ninja

How did this activity make YOU feel?

Add a thumbs up or a thumbs down sticker here.

Grumpy Ninja

Zen Ninja

ANXIOUS WORDS

Anxious Ninja has a challenge for you. Can you fill in words relating to anxiety? Each one should use at least one letter from the word ANXIOUS.

IDEAS TO TRY!
NERVOUS
EXHAUSTED

A
N
X
I
O
U
S

POSITIVELY AWESOME!

Here are some of the mantras that Anxious Ninja uses to help with anxious feelings. Why don't you give them a try? Color the hearts as you try each mantra, then rank them from 1 to 7, with 1 being the most helpful.

I am stronger than I think I am!

Nobody is perfect all the time!

It doesn't matter if I get it wrong, as long as I try!

I will always try my best!

If we all work together, we can achieve more!

Take a deep breath and focus!

I can do this!

Answers:

PAGE 16: WORD SEARCH

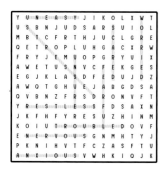

PAGE 17: DON'T BE LATE

PAGE 24: COLOR AND STICK

PAGE 26-27: SPOT THE DIFFERENCE

PAGE 30: DOT-TO-DOT

PAGE 38-39: SEARCH AND FIND

3   3   4   2   2   5   2   5   5   6

PAGES 42-43: RACE TIME

PAGE 44: WORD SEARCH

PAGE 47: SPOT THE DIFFERENCE

PAGE 56: WHAT DO YOU FEEL

Headache

Tense eyebrows

Grinding teeth

Clenched fists

Heavy breathing

Churning stomach

Racing heart

PAGE 57: CODE BREAKER
"TAKE A DEEP BREATH TO RELAX"

PAGE 60: ODD ONE OUT

PAGE 61: SHADOW MATCHING

PAGE 65: COLOR BY NUMBERS

PAGE 68: CHILL OUT

A.   B.   C.

PAGE 69: DOT-TO-DOT

PAGE 77: MATCHY-MATCHY
1 MATCHES THE BIG PICTURE

PAGE 13: MAKE A WORRY JAR

STORE YOUR WORRIES AWAY TILL ANOTHER DAY

MY WORRY JAR

PAGE 24: COLOR AND STICK

PAGES 26–27: SPOT THE DIFFERENCE

JUST FOR FUN STICKERS

PAGE 30: DOT-TO-DOT

EMOTION STICKERS: THROUGHOUT BOOK

PAGES 38-39: SEARCH AND FIND

PAGES 74-75: SILLY DRESS UP

EMOTION STICKERS: THROUGHOUT BOOK